Start Writing
About People and Places

Penny King
Ruth Thomson

Thameside Press

Distributed in the United States by
Smart Apple Media
1980 Lookout Drive
North Mankato, MN 56003

ISBN 1-930643-48-9

Library of Congress Control Number: 2001088839

Series editors: Mary-Jane Wilkins, Stephanie Turnbull
Designers: Rachel Hamdi, Holly Mann, Angie Allison
Illustrators: Beccy Blake, Kevin McAleenan, Melanie Mansfield, Lisa Smith
Educational consultants: Pie Corbett, Poet and Consultant
   to the English National Literacy Strategy; Sarah Mullen, Literacy Consultant

Printed in Spain

9 8 7 6 5 4 3 2 1

Contents

How to use this book

Do you know how to write a convincing ad, a thrilling account, or clear instructions?

This book will show you lots of different kinds of nonfiction writing.

HOUSE FOR SALE

What do you think of this ad? Does it make the house sound its best? How could it be improved?

> **FOR SALE**
> **295 Newtown Way**
> A great house in a terrible area. Any offers?

Maybe this ad will sell the house. It emphasizes good points and ignores bad ones. It appeals to as many people as possible.

Below is a list of good and bad points about the house.

Good points	Bad points
• Very big.	• Noisy planes.
• Fancy gate.	• Traffic fumes.
• Safe, neat yard.	• Graffiti.
• View of hills.	• Electricity pylon nearby.
• Shopping nearby.	• Smells from the dump.
• Lots of space.	• Could be rats!
• Good security.	• Needs more security.

Here are some people who might like this house.

Pilot (close to airport)

Gardening enthusiast (big yard)

Large family (lots of space and a yard)

Supermarket worker (could walk to work)

Truck driver (close to major highway)

A really boastful start.

Gardeners and families will like this.

There's no need to say how close!

People like bargains.

FOR SALE

295 Newtown Way

Magnificent family house with charming walled front yard and splendid iron gate.
Walking distance from local stores, roads, and transportation.
Handy for airport.
Interesting views.
Burglar alarm, automatic security gates, and entry phone.

Bargain price—$95,000

This can mean lots of bedrooms.

Sounds very grand.

This might interest pilots or business people.

This makes the house sound safe.

6

7

There are two double pages for each style of writing. The first one (see the example above) shows you how to plan your writing and gives you a model of a finished letter, ad, account, or chart.

Sometimes there are labels to help you, or a table like the one at the right.

Good points	Bad points
• Very big.	• Noisy planes.
• Fancy gate.	• Traffic fumes.
• Safe, neat yard.	• Graffiti.
• View of hills.	• Electricity pylon nearby.
• Shopping nearby.	• Smells from the dump.
• Lots of space.	• Could be rats!
• Good security.	• Needs more security.

The second double page (see the example below) gives you step-by-step instructions to create your own piece of writing.

Read the instructions carefully before you start writing.

Writing an ad

Write a tempting ad for one of these two places.

1 First make a list of good and bad points about it.

2 Think about who might want to live there and why.

3 Write FOR SALE at the top of your ad.

4 Write the address.

5 Describe the house and yard. Keep it short.

6 Give buyers an idea of what is nearby—shopping, transportation, landmarks.

7 Describe the view and any special features.

8 Say how much it costs.

WRITING TIPS

When you write an ad:

• use enthusiastic adjectives:

splendid	impressive	amazing
glorious	delightful	fabulous
stunning	luxurious	magnificent

• use appealing adjectives to cover up any faults:

cozy = tiny
interesting = strange
private = in the middle of nowhere
popular = expensive
extraordinary = you won't believe your eyes!

Rewrite this using what you have learned about writing ads.

FOR RENT
Apt. 236, Terror Towers

Filthy, tiny apartment with crumbling balcony on 13th floor. Deafening noise from dog pound and local amusement arcade. Trains almost pass through kitchen. Surrounded by huge construction site. Decorated entirely in black and red.

Overpriced at $1,000 per month

8   9

WRITING TIPS

The writing tips explain the particular rules for each style of writing.

The pictures are full of extra ideas to make your writing come to life.

Sometimes there is a box of useful verbs or adjectives.

Enthusiastic adjectives:

splendid	impressive	amazing
glorious	delightful	fabulous
stunning	luxurious	magnificent

You can either use these suggestions or think of other suitable words.

HOUSE FOR SALE

What do you think of this ad?
Does it make the house sound its best?
How could it be improved?

FOR SALE
295 Newtown Way

A great house
in a terrible area.

Any offers?

SUPERMARKET

FOR SALE

Below is a list of good and
bad points about the house.

Good points	Bad points
• Very big.	• Noisy planes.
• Fancy gate.	• Traffic fumes.
• Safe, neat yard.	• Graffiti.
• View of hills.	• Electricity pylon nearby.
• Shopping nearby.	• Smells from the dump.
• Lots of space.	• Could be rats!
• Good security.	• Needs more security.

Here are some people
who might like this house.

Pilot (close to airport)

Gardening enthusiast (big yard)

Large family (lots of space and a yard)

Supermarket worker (could walk to work)

Truck driver (close to major highway)

Maybe this ad will sell the house. It emphasizes good points and ignores bad ones. It appeals to as many people as possible.

A really boastful start.

This can mean lots of bedrooms.

Gardeners and families will like this.

Sounds very grand.

There's no need to say how close!

This might interest pilots or business people.

People like bargains.

This makes the house sound safe.

FOR SALE
295 Newtown Way

Magnificent family house
with charming walled front yard
and splendid iron gate.
Walking distance from local stores,
roads, and transportation.
Handy for airport.
Interesting views.
Burglar alarm, automatic security
gates, and entry phone.

Bargain price—$95,000

Writing an ad

Write a tempting ad for one of these two places.

1 First make a list of good and bad points about it.

2 Think about who might want to live there and why.

3 Write FOR SALE at the top of your ad.

4 Write the address.

5 Describe the house and yard. Keep it short.

6 Give buyers an idea of what is nearby—shopping, transportation, landmarks.

7 Describe the view and any special features.

8 Say how much it costs.

WRITING TIPS

When you write an ad:

• use enthusiastic adjectives:

splendid	impressive	amazing
glorious	delightful	fabulous
stunning	luxurious	magnificent

• use appealing adjectives to cover up any faults:

cozy = tiny

interesting = strange

private = in the middle of nowhere

popular = expensive

extraordinary = you won't believe
your eyes!

Rewrite this using what you have learned about writing ads.

FOR RENT

Apt. 236, Terror Towers

Filthy, tiny apartment with crumbling balcony on 13th floor. Deafening noise from dog pound and local amusement arcade. Trains almost pass through kitchen. Surrounded by huge construction site. Decorated entirely in black and red.

Overpriced at $1,000 per month

PACKING UP

Mrs. Jones is moving. She has many precious possessions to pack.
This calls for some clear instructions.

Imagine wrapping this valuable pot. Think about what you would do and in what order.

Here is one way to pack the pot safely.
You may have thought of a different way.
It doesn't matter, as long as the pot is safe.

How to pack a pot

You will need:

- newspaper
- bubble wrap
- strong tape
- strong cardboard box
- styrofoam chips
- marker

What you do:

1 Remove the lid and make sure the pot is empty.

2 Stuff the pot with crumpled-up newspaper.

3 Wrap the pot—first with newspaper, then with bubble wrap.

4 Use strong tape to keep the wrapping in place.

5 Wrap the lid in newspaper and tape it to the top of the pot.

6 Crumple up some newspaper and put a layer in the cardboard box.

7 Put the pot carefully in the box.

8 Fill the box with styrofoam chips and bubble wrap.

9 Close the box with strong tape.

10 Label the box **FRAGILE**.

Writing instructions

Write clear instructions for packing one of these items.

A huge glass tank full of fierce fish

Lots of frozen food

1 First think about how you would wrap the object.

2 Write the title:
How to pack a...

3 Write the heading:
You will need

4 List the materials you need. Write them in the order that you will use them.

5 Write the heading:
What you do

6 Write exactly what to do, step by step.

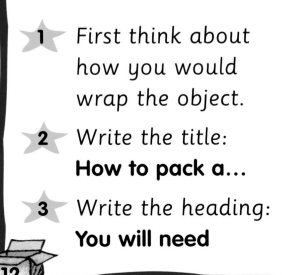

A set of delicate china

A fancy glass chandelier

WRITING TIPS

When you write instructions:

- write in the present tense.
- only describe one activity at a time.
- number each instruction.
- begin each instruction with a verb.
- start each instruction on a new line.

Use bossy verbs (imperatives) to explain exactly what to do.

place	use	protect	roll
label	fill	wrap	unscrew
stick	take	cover	remove
stuff	pack	empty	crumple

POINTS OF VIEW

What do you think about doing homework? Do your parents think the same? Does your teacher agree?

What do your friends think? The best way to find out everyone's opinion about homework is to ask them.

I'm tired after school, so I can't concentrate on homework.

Me

Homework keeps you out of mischief!

Grandma

I try to help you, but I just confuse you—I don't know how things are taught at your school.

Mom

Doing homework helps you learn to get organized and remember what to bring home.

Dad

When you have homework you don't have time to play with me.

Little brother

It's good for you to work alone, so I can see what you understand.

I can't go to Sports Club because of all my homework.

Teacher

Best friend

You can put people's opinions on a "For" and "Against" chart like this.

Write this at the top of the left-hand column.

Write the statement at the top.

Write this at the top of the right-hand column.

Children should do homework.

For	Against
• Children practice what they learn at school. • Children learn more. • Children learn how to get organized. • Children are kept busy. • Children are more confident because they have learned things well.	• Children are very tired and can't do their best. • Parents may confuse children by explaining things in the wrong way. • Children don't have time for playing or their hobbies.

Start each new reason with a bullet point.

End by writing about what you think and why.

I think that children should do homework because it helps them learn.

For and against

Choose one of the statements on these pages. Think of reasons for and against it. The pictures give you some ideas.

1 First do some research. You might:
- interview people you know.
- write to people.
- make a questionnaire.

2 Next make a chart. Put the statement at the top. Divide the page in half. Write "For" in one column and "Against" in the other.

3 Write as many reasons as you can in each column.

4 End with a conclusion saying what you think and why.

All children should be given an allowance.

Children should do sports every day.

WRITING TIPS

When you write your chart:

- start each opinion with a bullet point.

- when you write an opinion, try to think of the opposite view too.

- give a reason for your final decision: "I think that... because..."

ALL ABOUT ANIMALS

Reports are factual. They explain the way things are. This information about penguins is from an animal handbook.

BIRDS Emperor Penguin

HABITAT

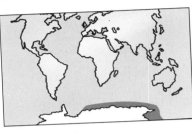

Emperor Penguins live in seas around Antarctica, in large groups called flocks.

APPEARANCE

The Emperor Penguin is the largest of all penguins.
Height: 3 3/4 ft.
Weight: 65 lbs.

Small bill

Oily, waterproof feathers

Thick blubber keeps penguin warm

Wings used for swimming not flying

Small feet

Tail steers when bird is swimming

BREEDING

In the fall, male and female penguins travel 60 miles south to a nesting site. There, they meet a lifelong mate. Three weeks later, the female lays one egg. She returns north to feed, leaving the male to care for the egg.

The male keeps the egg warm on his feet under a flap of skin. He does this for two months. He eats nothing and huddles together with other males to keep warm. When the egg hatches, the female returns to feed the chick. The male can feed at last.

FEEDING

Penguins are fast swimmers (up to 18 miles per hour). They catch fish, squid, and krill in their beaks, and eat underwater.

This report is based on the information and pictures found in the handbook.

Emperor Penguins

Emperor penguins have black heads, wings, and feet and white stomachs. Their necks are bright yellow. They are the biggest of all the penguins.

They live in Antarctica, which is a very cold place. They have waterproof feathers to keep dry and fat to keep warm.

Penguins have wings but they cannot fly, though they swim fast. They use their wings like flippers and steer with their tails. They catch their food while they are swimming.

Wings push them forward

Tail steers

Krill

Squid

In the fall, penguins travel to nesting sites. The female penguin lays one white egg. The male puts it on top of his feet to keep it warm. The female goes away to eat. The male penguins stand close together to keep warm. They do not eat for two months. The female returns when the egg hatches, and then the male can eat. Baby penguins are called chicks.

egg

egg cracks

chick

I saw some chicks at the zoo. They had soft, fluffy, gray feathers instead of black and white ones. The mother was feeding them with fish straight from her mouth into theirs. Most people love penguins, and we need to protect them.

What they look like

Where they live

What they do

What they eat

Their babies

Writer's own comments

A good ending

Writing a report

Write a report about giant pandas or African elephants.

MAMMALS Giant Panda

HABITAT

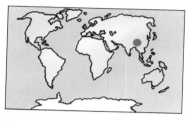

Pandas live alone in the cold, high bamboo forests in the mountains of China.

BREEDING

Female pandas produce one or two babies (cubs) every two or three years. Cubs weigh only about 3½ ounces and have no fur. Cubs need a lot of care and usually only one survives.

FEEDING

Pandas live mostly on bamboo shoots and roots. Sometimes they eat small animals, birds, and fish. Adult pandas eat up to 85 lbs. of bamboo each day.

APPEARANCE

Height: 5½ ft.
Weight: Up to 330 lbs.

Eyes have good night vision

Powerful jaws

Thick fur

Hairy feet for walking on snow and ice

Large paws for grabbing shoots and roots

Sharp claws

⭐ **1** First read the information. Look up any words you do not understand in a dictionary.

⭐ **2** Make a list of the following questions and jot down the answers as you find them.

- What does the animal look like?
- Where does it live?
- What does it eat?
- What do you know about its babies?

MAMMALS African Elephant

HABITAT

Elephants live in large groups called herds on the grassy plains of Africa.

APPEARANCE

Height: 12 ft.
Weight: Up to 7 ½ tonnes

BREEDING

Females (cows) give birth to one baby (calf) every four or five years. The calves weigh 200 lbs. and are 3 feet tall. They drink their mother's milk until they are six years old.

FEEDING

Elephants spend up to 18 hours a day grazing on grasses, leaves, roots, tree bark, and fruit. An adult can eat up to 500 lbs. of food and drink 50 gallons of water every day.

Large ears flap to cool elephant

Thick skin

Tail swishes flies away

Long trunk for smelling, sucking up water, and picking up things

Tusks for digging and fighting

3 The neat copy. Write the title.

4 Write your report using the answers to your questions.

5 Add facts of your own. Look in other books to make sure they are correct.

> WRITING TIPS

When you write a report:

- write in the present tense.
- start a new paragraph for every answer.
- end with a short conclusion.

21

WHERE AM I?

Imagine that you have just arrived at this town's train station. You are going to meet a friend at the movies.

Your friend has given you some directions and a map. Read the directions and trace your route on the map.

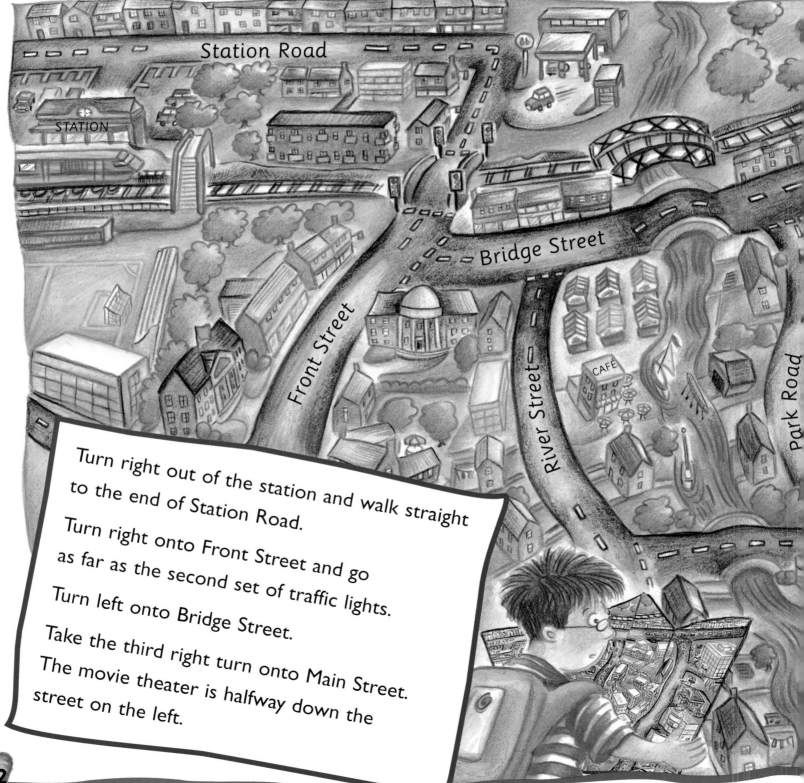

Station Road

STATION

Bridge Street

Front Street

River Street

CAFÉ

Park Road

Turn right out of the station and walk straight to the end of Station Road.

Turn right onto Front Street and go as far as the second set of traffic lights.

Turn left onto Bridge Street.

Take the third right turn onto Main Street. The movie theater is halfway down the street on the left.

Writing directions

Now write directions
from the movie theater
to the café by the river.
Use these steps to help you.

1 Find the movie theater and the café. Trace the route between them with your finger.

Pretend you are starting with your back to the theater—then you won't mix up your rights and lefts!

2 Write directions using bossy verbs (imperatives) such as:

turn	take
cross	go straight down
follow	walk

3 Every time the route changes direction, write a new instruction on a new line.

HOSPITAL

Main Street

MOVIE THEATER

POLICE

> WRITING TIPS

When you write directions:

- always use street names where possible.

- mention useful landmarks such as a police station, a gas station, a hospital, a park, or a school.

MY AMAZING NEWS

Everyone loves to talk about something exciting that has happened to them.

These pictures show the main events of a family's adventure in the snow. Can you recount what happened?

1

2

3

4

First look at the pictures. What is the setting, and who are the people? What happens first, next, and later? How does the adventure end?

Here is one way of writing an imaginative account of the events.

Adventure in the snow

Last Sunday we were driving home from Grandma's house. It started snowing. After an hour the snow was really heavy. Dad couldn't see where he was going. The car started sliding on the road. Sally was scared and so was I. Suddenly the car skidded off the road and crashed into a tree. It sounded like an explosion. Mom screamed. Luckily none of us was hurt.

After that we got out of the car to see what had happened to it. The front was dented and the engine would not start.

Next we walked down the road to find a phone. I was so cold that my feet felt like blocks of ice. The snow blew into my eyes, so I could hardly see a thing. No cars came by and we didn't see a single phone.

Finally we came to a house. We ran to the door and knocked as hard as we could. The woman who lived there let us use her phone to call a tow truck. She said we looked like a family of snowmen! She gave us some hot chocolate while we waited.

Mom and Dad said we had both been really brave about the crash and the snowy walk.

25

Writing an account

Choose a set of pictures and write an action-packed account.

1. Decide who to be.
2. Look at the pictures. Figure out what happens and how it ends.
3. Think of a title.
4. Write about the pictures in order. Start a new paragraph for each picture.
5. End by making a comment about what happened.

1

2

3

4

⚑ WRITING TIPS

When you write an account:

- use words like after, later, and next to give your reader an idea of when things happened.

- describe your feelings at each stage to make your account even more interesting.

A DREAM JOB

Imagine that you have stepped back in time. You see this ad. What sort of letter would you write to persuade Captain Scott to take you with him?

Ed Venture made a list of his skills and talents.

WANTED!
Exceptional people
for the
adventure of a lifetime.
Expedition on foot
to
The South Pole

Apply in writing to:
Captain Robert Falcon Scott

Determined and brave

Excellent cook

Strong swimmer

Fit and healthy

Champion skier

Enthusiastic camper

Animal expert

Experienced fisherman

Skilled navigator

I hope he chooses me!

Ed Venture used his list to write a persuasive letter to Captain Scott.

He included as many reasons as possible to show why he was the best person for the job.

Begins with "Dear..."

Address in the top right-hand corner

Hill Farm
Willoughby
New Hampshire
January 25, 1909

Date under address

Dear Captain Scott,

I see from your ad that you are looking for exceptional people to travel with you to the South Pole.

I am 24 years old and very fit and healthy. I am an experienced fisherman and love being at sea. I am a very strong swimmer. While on the night watch I taught myself to navigate, using the stars. I am also an excellent cook.

Lists things he can do

I am sure it would be useful to have someone on your expedition who can look after animals. I am used to caring for animals and know cures for many common illnesses. I therefore think I would be a great help to you.

I have always dreamed of exploring unknown places, especially snowy ones, since I love to camp and ski.

Yours sincerely,

Ed Venture

This Ed Venture sounds just right for the job!

Uses persuasive language

Ends with this

Signs his name

29

Applying for a job

Which of these two jobs would you prefer?

Can you think of reasons why you should be chosen? Don't be shy—sing your own praises!

WANTED!
Brave pilot
to be a navigator
on
an exciting
around-the-world flight.

Apply in writing to: Ms. Amelia Earhart

Write a letter to one of these people from the past. Try to persuade them that you are the right person for the job.

1 First think of all the reasons why you are right for the job.

2 Write your address and the date in the right-hand corner.

3 Start the letter with "Dear...".

WANTED!

Actors

able to

sing, dance, and perform

in the plays of

Mr. William Shakespeare

at a

London Theater

Apply in writing to: Mr. Richard Burbage

4 ★ Say who you are and write a little about each of your good points.

5 ★ End with "Yours sincerely".

6 ★ Sign your full name.

WRITING TIPS

When you write your letter:

- use persuasive language to convince the person that you are ideal for the job.

- only list skills that are useful for the job.